Lucinda's Magical Yoga Adventure

Written by Betty Larrea
Illustrations by Lorena Isabel

Published by Be Yoga Be Love Press
Printed by Signature Book Printing. Inc.

ISBN: 978-0-578-15146-5

For instructional guide to each yoga pose featured in this book and to inquire about book readings, parties and special events, please visit author website at www.bettylarrea.com.

For information on Be Yoga Be Love educational programs and professional training, please visit www.beyogabelove.com.

Dear Parents,

Lucinda's Magical Yoga Adventure combines my love for both yoga and poetry. I am excited to share this book with you and your child, so that you may experience the magic of yoga together. Like Lucinda, children love to pretend to *become* the animals and characters they meet on their yoga adventure.

Having taught yoga to hundreds of children, I have witnessed the benefits that yoga provides in their lives. I see how they blossom as they become aware of their gifts and find their own unique expression. My wish is that when your children read this book, their imaginations will run free and they will discover their connection to themselves and the world around them.

Namaste (*The Light in Me Honors the Light in You*)

Betty

Hi! I'm Lucinda and I love yoga.

When I'm doing yoga
I can pretend to be
A dog, a cat, a mountain
Or anything I want to be

On my yoga adventure
I'm always sure to find
Many fun and playful ways
to calm my body and my mind

I wished upon a shooting star
for a magic wand that
makes any dream come true
Come test its magical powers with me!

I grab onto the string of a Big Balloon
When I tap it with my magic wand,
the balloon lifts me up into the sky
I wonder, "Where am I going?"

I am like a big balloon
Filling up as I breathe in
When I let my breath go out
I find a quiet place within

I land in an Enchanted Forest
Look! Here's a fuzzy caterpillar
When I wave my magic wand...
It turns into a Beautiful Butterfly!

I am like a butterfly
Flapping my wings up high
I'm free to be the way I am
as I'm soaring in the sky

While skipping through the forest,
I see a trail of glittery seeds
My magic wand turns them into
a garden of Fanciful Flowers!

I am like a pretty flower
My petals spread out wide
Lifting high upon my stem
I show my beauty from inside

Walking through the beautiful garden,
I find a bone on the ground
One wave of my magic wand...
Poof! it becomes a Delightful Dog.

I am like a happy dog
My paws pressed to the ground
I wag my tail and bark out loud
as I'm sniffing all around

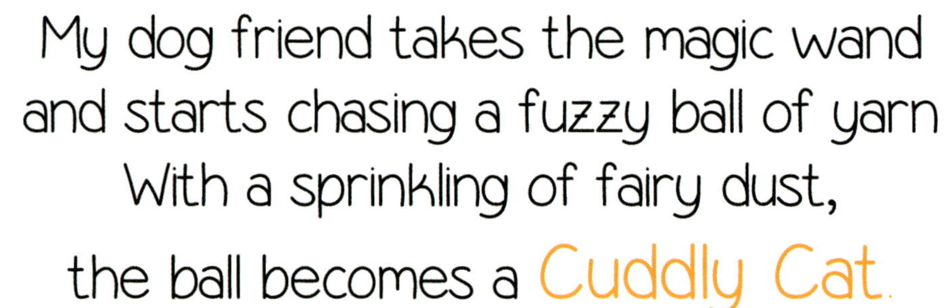

My dog friend takes the magic wand
and starts chasing a fuzzy ball of yarn
With a sprinkling of fairy dust,
the ball becomes a Cuddly Cat.

I am like a kitty cat
Stretched out across the floor
It feels so good to arch my back
and then stretch out some more

We stop to cool off by a small pond
I take my wand and go Swoosh!
All the lily pads floating on the water
turn into Fabulous Frogs.

I am like a friendly frog
Jumping up into the air
I flick my tongue to catch some flies
as I hop from here to there

After playing with the froggies,
I need a quiet place to rest
I use my wand to turn some leaves
into a Tall Tree to sit against.

I am like a growing tree
My trunk is tall and long
I raise my arms like branches
So I can balance and be strong

While I'm resting, a twig falls from the tree
When it touches my wand, I look up
I'm surprised to see a Silly Snake
crawling up the tree's trunk.

I am like a cobra snake
Slithering all around
I move and twist my body
as I make a hissing sound

It's time to go home now...
On my way back, I meet a Loony Lion
He peeks out from the bushes
and asks "Will you be my friend?"

I am like a mighty lion
Watch me crouch down low
I pounce and leap into the air
Roaring loudly as I go

When we reach the water,
We need a way to go across
I use my wand to build a Big Bridge
which leads us back home.

I am like a sturdy bridge
Stretching out over the sea
I lift up from my center
With my hands under me

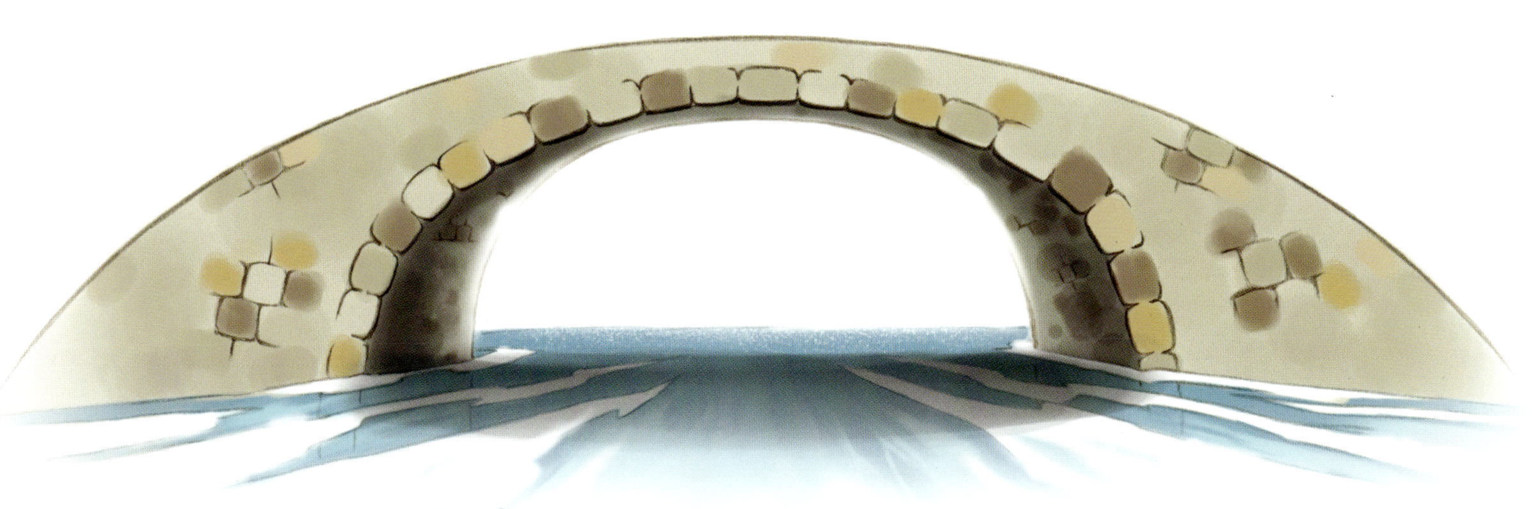

It's been such a long day
As I lay in bed, drifting off to sleep
A Comfy Cloud lifts me into Dreamland...
"Where will we go next?"

Where will you go?
Who will you get to be?
Now that you love yoga
just as much as me!

This book is dedicated to my niece, soul sister and BFF.

Armanni,

Since the day you were born, you've brought so much love and laughter to me and our whole family. Thank you for reminding me how much I love to PLAY! Your free spirit, creativity and imagination inspired me to write this book. Always remember to keep shining your beautiful light in the world!

I Love You!

Auntie B

Acknowledgements

My heart is overflowing with love and gratitude for all the people who were such an important part of making my dream of being a published author come true.

Mom: For your love, endless support and generosity. You have been my greatest cheerleader throughout this entire journey of birthing my book into the world!

Dad: For teaching me to work hard and never give up on my dreams. You have always believed in me and encouraged me to share the gift of my writing.

Wil (my lil' bro): For all your time, feedback and creative input throughout the illustration process AND for bringing my beautiful nieces into the world to inspire me.

Alice: For always seeing and accepting me for who I am. You are my North Star, spiritual mother and evolutionary partner.

Sirena: For being my magical guide and holding the space for me to fully embody my Soul's purpose of bringing love and authenticity to others through PLAY!

Lorena: For capturing the whimsy and spirit I envisioned for my book in each and every illustration. You infused so much love and life into Lucinda that she seems to jump off the page!

Duncan Ewald, Ted Enik, Scott and Judie: For seeing the potential in my story and taking the time to review my manuscript.

Jen, Becky, and Nayeli: For being my teachers and mentors as I continue to deepen my own yoga practice.

And to all the children I've taught over the past 13 years: For teaching me to PLAY YOGA. Your sense of wonder and imagination bring me so much love and joy every single day!

About the Author-Betty Larrea

I am a writer, yoga instructor, educator, artist, poet and nature lover. My greatest passion is inspiring others to love and express who they are in the world. Play has been the gateway to my authentic self and I infuse a little bit of play into everything I do! I've been writing stories and poetry since I was a child and I love playing with words.

I am also a Yoga Alliance Registered Yoga Teacher and have been teaching yoga to children since 2001. In 2010, I founded *Be Yoga Be Love* and I'm currently providing my curriculum, staff development training, and event services for children and educators in schools, libraries, and yoga studios throughout NJ and NY. I love to read, write, create, dance, explore and discover the wonder in each moment.

About the Illustrator- Lorena Isabel

I am a visual artist living and working in Buenos Aires, Argentina. I have loved art and drawing from a very young age. Since embracing illustration and animation as a lifestyle in 1997, I have been creating illustrated books and animated films locally and abroad. I am currently involved in doing commissioned work, while pursuing my own personal projects.

I have always had a special connection with characters driven by the spirit of play and wonder, so working on this book has been such a delightful journey for me. I hope you, as the reader, enjoy the words and art in this book as much as I enjoyed bringing Lucinda to life.